J   Tools of Combat (Warri
623   Chambers,Catherin
CHA   9.99   36103

DATE DUE

J   Tools of Combat (Warri
623   Chambers,Catherin
CHA   9.99   36103

DATE	ISSUED TO
5/8/19	Coggins
10/1/19	ABC

WARRIORS!
TOOLS OF COMBAT

Thanks to the creative team:
Senior Editor: Alice Peebles
Design: www.collaborate.agency
Consultant: John Haywood

Hungry Tomato™
A division of Lerner Publishing Group, Inc.
241 First Avenue North
Minneapolis, MN 55401 USA

For reading levels and more information, look up this title at www.lernerbooks.com.

Main body text set in Bell MT.
Typeface provided by Monotype.

Library of Congress Cataloging-in-Publication Data

Chambers, Catherine, 1954– author.
Tools of combat / by Catherine Chambers.
    pages cm. — (Warriors!)
Includes bibliographical references and index.
Audience: Grades 4-6.
ISBN 978-1-4677-9355-1 (lb : alk. paper) — ISBN 978-1-4677-9597-5 (pb : alk. paper) — ISBN 978-1-4677-9598-2 (eb pdf)
1. Weapons—History—Juvenile literature. 2. Swords—History—Juvenile literature. I. Title.
U810.C53 2016
623.4'4–dc23

2015027940

Manufactured in the United States of America
1 – VP – 12/31/15

WARRIORS!
TOOLS OF COMBAT

by Catherine Chambers
Illustrated by Martín Bustamante

HUNGRY
TOMATO™

CONTENTS

INTRODUCING METAL WEAPONS

Most metals are tough and easily shaped and sharpened. Blacksmiths and swordsmiths could smelt, mold, hammer, and grind bronze, iron, and steel to make the deadliest handheld weapons. Some were thick, heavy bludgeoning instruments. Others were slender, fine, lethally sharp spikes and blades. Yet others could hook a knight off his horse or pin him to the ground. From fine arrowheads to slashing swords, sharp metal weapons carried by soldiers dominated warfare until modern times.

WEAPONS AND ARMOR

A spear or arrow has a head with a tip, attached to an arm, or shaft.

A sword or dagger has a blade with a sharp tip at the end. The handle is called a hilt, often ending in a ball-shaped pommel. The hilt's cross guard is known as a quillon.

A mace (above left), axe, or hammering weapon has a head attached to a handle, or haft.

Mail was the earliest form of armor for a medieval knight. It consisted of tens of thousands of interlocking metal rings woven together to form a shirt, or hauberk, for the body and a coif for the head.

PERSONAL PROTECTION

Armor strengthened as metal weapons became more deadly. Metal weapons became even more deadly as armor strengthened! Mail made from small metal links enabled the soldier to move with some ease. But a sword tip, dagger, or arrow could force its way through.

Plate armor *(right)* began to replace mail around 1200. Shaped from sheets of metal, it gave better protection against crush injuries. But the articulated joints made to fit the limbs could still be pierced by a sharp weapon. Shields might be bashed or unhooked from a soldier's arm. Battleaxes, hammers, and flails were used to bludgeon helmets—and heads.

TOP TRAINING

Training with a lance included attacking a dummy and shield tied high on a swinging pole. The trainee galloped in fast and tried to hit the target hard.

SUPER SKILLS

Pikes were heavy, with 75 percent of their weight held in front. A soldier had to develop great strength to hold the pike straight, without letting it dip.

MIGHTY MATERIALS

The heavy, tapered pole shaft was made from a strong wood such as ash. Near its end, the shaft was often strengthened further with iron sleeves, called cheeks.

FEROCIOUS FACTS

● The pike's length ranged from 6 to 21 ft (2 to 6.5 m).

● Pike heads might have a deadly tip, axe head, and hook.

● Sharp lance points could pierce plate armor.

PIERCING PIKES AND LANCES

The pike was a long, savage spear in use from the earliest times. Its extreme length enabled a soldier to make the first strike. Its razor-sharp, leaf-shaped steel tip wounded an opponent viciously and often fatally. Soldiers marched or ran with their pikes in a close formation, called a phalanx *(left)*. Like a massive, surging bed of nails, the phalanx stopped the enemy in its tracks. A spear wielded by fast-moving cavalry was called a lance. At speed, this weapon could inflict a deadly wound or knock an opponent from his horse.

WHERE
Europe, Asia, North Africa

WHEN
300 BCE to 1600s —based on earlier spears used worldwide

- Shaft or pole of hardwood
- Metal tips in various shapes, all very hard and sharp

LETHAL LONGBOW

WHERE

From the British Isles
to Northern Europe

WHEN

1100 to 1600s

The English longbow fired sharp, barbed iron arrows far and fast. The bow was so strong that an arrow could kill from 900 ft (274 m) away. The longbow's strength came from its height. At 6 ft (1.8 m) long it was as tall as a man, and its long string could be pulled back like a powerful catapult. Thin arrows pierced straight through a soldier's mail, while broader, heavier arrows flew farther and higher into a line of approaching infantry or cavalry. In battle, thousands of archers might advance in rows, raining down a storm of arrows on their enemy. More often, they fought defensively behind a line of sharpened stakes.

- Bow stave, often made of yew
- Hemp or flax bowstring
- Feather fletching, or flight, to stabilize the arrow

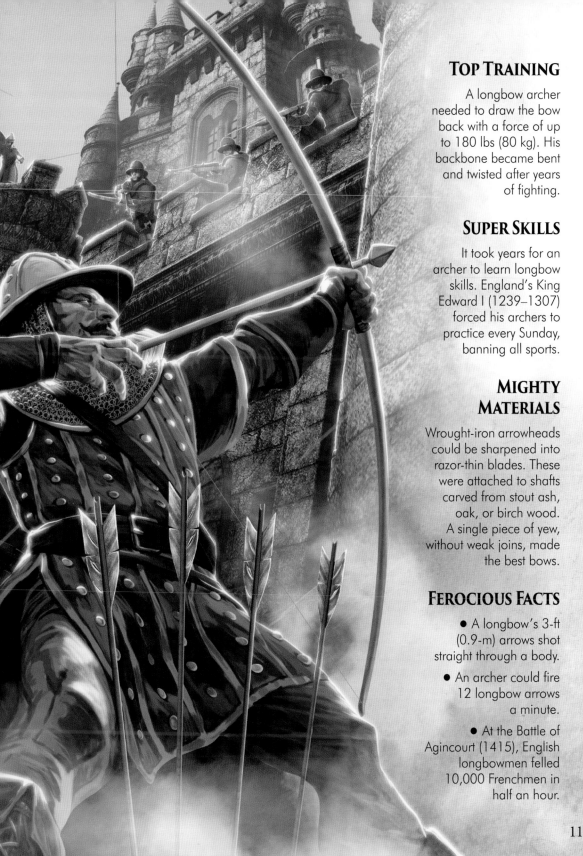

TOP TRAINING

A longbow archer needed to draw the bow back with a force of up to 180 lbs (80 kg). His backbone became bent and twisted after years of fighting.

SUPER SKILLS

It took years for an archer to learn longbow skills. England's King Edward I (1239–1307) forced his archers to practice every Sunday, banning all sports.

MIGHTY MATERIALS

Wrought-iron arrowheads could be sharpened into razor-thin blades. These were attached to shafts carved from stout ash, oak, or birch wood. A single piece of yew, without weak joins, made the best bows.

FEROCIOUS FACTS

- A longbow's 3-ft (0.9-m) arrows shot straight through a body.

- An archer could fire 12 longbow arrows a minute.

- At the Battle of Agincourt (1415), English longbowmen felled 10,000 Frenchmen in half an hour.

11

TOP TRAINING

A young knight practiced by thrusting and slashing a pell, or stout wooden post, set firmly into the ground. He learned how to angle and strike with both edges of the blade.

SUPER SKILLS

A soldier with a longsword had no free arm to help balance his body as he thrust and cut. Instead, he developed strength in his legs and upper body for greater control.

MIGHTY MATERIALS

The longsword was very tough. A swordsmith heated and hammered strips of iron continually to strengthen them. He gave the sword balance by varying the width and thickness along the length of the blade.

FEROCIOUS FACTS

- The blade measured up to 48 in (122 cm) long, reaching from the floor to a soldier's chest.

- It could sever a limb or head in one stroke.

- The hilt's pommel and quillon were used to bash the opponent.

LOPPING WITH LONGSWORDS

This savage sword was a foot soldier's or knight's close-combat weapon of war. It had a strong, straight, double-edged blade with a long reach and a pointed tip. But its main advantage over other swords was its extended hilt. This enabled the soldier to grip tightly with both hands, increasing his power and control. He thrust at and pierced the opponent's mail forcefully from a distance. Or he cut and sliced at plate armor and exposed limbs— or neck! He bore down on an opponent's weapon, knocking it out of his hands. The sword also allowed for fast, strong strikes with one hand by a fighter on horseback.

WHERE
Central and Northern Europe

WHEN
About 1250 to 1550

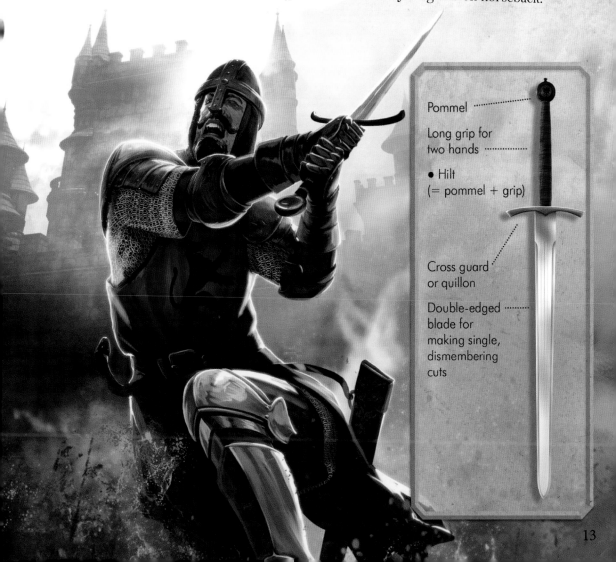

Pommel

Long grip for two hands

• Hilt (= pommel + grip)

Cross guard or quillon

Double-edged blade for making single, dismembering cuts

SLICING WITH THE SZABLA

WHERE

Central Europe

———•◆•———

WHEN

1600s to 1800s
—based on 6th-century
sabers from the
Middle East

A winged Polish hussar used one hand to slice and slash with his slender, shallow-curved szabla. Its blade's single, razor-sharp edge tapered to a long, double-edged, pointed tip. Every part of the blade could cut deeply, while the hilt inflicted a bruising blow. The hilt was crucial to the success of this sword. Its curve made it easy to grip, which allowed the swordsman to deliver a very firm, controlled, swift strike. The szabla might have a knuckle guard and thumb ring to protect the hand, and they could also give an opponent's hand a hefty strike.

Strengthend join (between blade and hilt)

Curved blade with one sharp edge

Double-edged tip, 6–7 in (15–18 cm) long

TOP TRAINING

Training included slashing while balancing on a swift horse. On the ground, a soldier practiced fast, short steps in all directions, learning to slice with the szabla from any angle. Keeping a straight back gave power to the strike.

SUPER SKILLS

Hussars changed their handgrip with lightning speed. They could suddenly push their thumb hard against the hilt, straightening the wrist, to deliver a fearsome strike.

MIGHTY MATERIALS

A szabla was made from fine, strong steel. The join between its hilt and blade was strengthened by two feather-shaped pieces of metal. The sword's long tip did not snap off easily.

FEROCIOUS FACTS

- The blade reached 33 in (85 cm), or from floor to hip, and could make a wide gash.

- Its curved edge inflicted "moulinets": painful circular cuts.

- Hussars wore wooden wings covered in feathers to create awe and fear.

15

TOP TRAINING

From five years old, samurai trained constantly with weapons, concentrating on swift movement and perfect judgment of distance. Thrusting and hitting had to be done with pinpoint accuracy.

SUPER SKILLS

Gunsen were carried in a sheath, with the fan tips uppermost. In a sudden attack, a samurai could withdraw the gunsen swiftly by its tips so that it unfolded, protecting his hand.

MIGHTY MATERIALS

War fans had between 6 and 13 sharpened metal or heavy wooden ribs held together with strong rivets. Gunsen could fold because the ribs were joined together with flexible paper.

FEROCIOUS FACTS

• Gunbai could span 20 in (51 cm) and kill with a blow.

• The gunsen's sharp paper folds inflicted cuts to the eyes.

• Samurai officers signaled secret tactics to their troops with their gunbai.

GASHING WITH THE GUNSEN AND GUNBAI

These Japanese war fans did more than keep samurai warriors cool! Gunsen were lightweight folding fans with sharp iron blades that could fend off stones, darts, and other small missiles. A gunbai was larger and heavier, and did not fold. It was designed as a fearsome defensive, controlling weapon. It parried, or blocked, a samurai opponent's sword. Or it dealt painful blows to the hand, elbow, or shoulder, forcing an enemy to drop his weapon. Fans aimed at the body's pressure points could paralyze. Once disarmed, the enemy was open to the samurai's deadly attack.

WHERE
Japan

WHEN
1400s to 1800s

- Varying number of metal ribs

- Paper, sometimes lacquered, attached to the ribs for folding the gunsen

SLASHING WITH THE SHAMSHIR

This slender, curved, single-edged sword was designed to slash an opponent rather than pierce him. In Persian, *shamshir* means "lion's claw" and well describes this fearsome crescent-shaped saber. Its strong central spine and long, tapering tip enabled the swordsman to slice with force. The lightweight shamshir was the Persian cavalry's deadliest single-handed weapon. Worn at the hip, it was drawn from a scabbard hung from two slings. It was perfect for fast-moving mounted warfare because it could be swung at enemy foot soldiers and cavalry in sweeping, carving movements.

... Inlaid hilt

Pronounced
curve to the
blade

Strong spine

Extended tip

TOP TRAINING

The sons of Persia's warrior class trained from an early age to ride horses and master swordsmanship. They perfected the technique of angling the sharp shamshir blade to inflict a deep slice.

SUPER SKILLS

An expert swordsman could aim accurately and fatally at the neck and around the waist near the kidneys. He could strike backward as well as forward.

MIGHTY MATERIALS

The best *wootz* steel from Damascus was used to make the finest blades. Wootz steel is also called watered steel because of its shimmering look. Gold, silver, and ivory inlays decorated the hilt.

FEROCIOUS FACTS

- The blade was up to 3 ft (0.9 m) long.
- It could chop at bones as well as slice at flesh.
- The curved pommel gave a firm grip for a powerful hit.

TOP TRAINING

The young sons of samurai attended special combat schools. Vital skills included withdrawing and controlling the katana, standing with balanced readiness, and glaring at the enemy.

SUPER SKILLS

Swordsmen could reverse the blade at great speed to strike from left to right, as well as right to left. A sudden thrust straight at the throat could surprise an enemy—fatally.

MIGHTY MATERIALS

Skilled swordsmiths heated and hammered together four layers of metal to make the blade. They used a tough but brittle steel for the razor-sharp edge. Layers of hard iron prevented the katana from bending, while a softer layer kept it from breaking.

FEROCIOUS FACTS

● The blade could measure up to 28.5 in (72 cm), or from floor to mid-thigh.

● The sloping, tapered tip enabled a complete gash to be made from an enemy's head to stomach.

● A braided cord around the hilt gave a firm grip to allow for a ferocious slash.

CUTTING WITH THE KILLER KATANA

This slender, two-handed sword was the main battle weapon of ruling samurai warriors. Its slightly curved, vicious, single-edged blade and sloping point were designed to slice in a circular, sweeping motion. A mounted samurai could draw the sword at great speed from a sash belt tied around the waist. The blade was held uppermost, so with one slick, quick movement he could grasp the hilt and slash the enemy. The hilt was straight and long, easily gripped with both hands.

WHERE
Japan

WHEN
1100s to 1800s

..... Extended grip for two hands

Circular or squared cross guard

Slightly curved blade made from layers of metal

WHACKING WITH THE WAR HAMMER

WHERE

Eastern, Central, and
Northern Europe

—◆•◆—

WHEN

1200s to 1400s
—based on earlier
Asian weapons

The foot soldiers of medieval armies wielded this fearsome, heavy weapon. Its purpose was to bash in helmets and breastplates, once plate armor became more widely used. A single blow from the hammerhead could knock an enemy unconscious, even through his helmet. It could splinter his skull, causing severe brain damage, and kill him. The sharp end or spike could tangle a horse's reins or unhook a knight's weapons, throwing him to the ground. It might pierce thinner metal joints, as well as mail and unprotected flesh. The war hammer's haft was also used defensively, to block sword strikes.

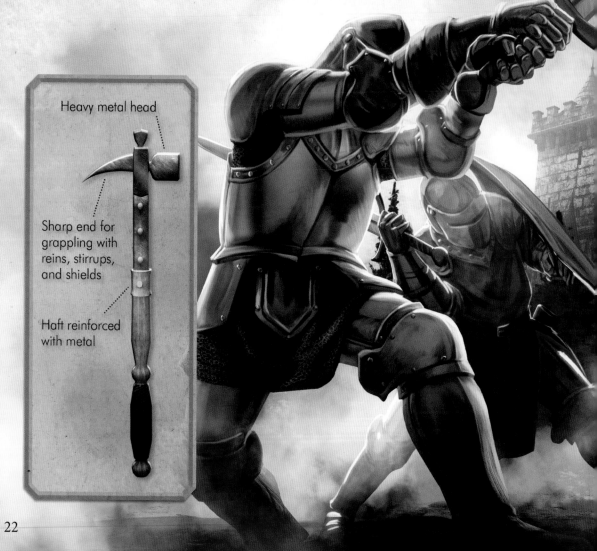

Heavy metal head

Sharp end for
grappling with
reins, stirrups,
and shields

Haft reinforced
with metal

TOP TRAINING

To aim accurately at a moving head with a long-hafted hammer, soldiers had to practice hitting a small target while running. They used lightweight wooden hammers to practice against fellow soldiers.

SUPER SKILLS

A skilled soldier could switch swiftly from hammer to blade. He developed strength in his arms so he could wield the war hammer with one hand and another weapon with the other.

MIGHTY MATERIALS

Army blacksmiths smelted and molded iron, steel, or very heavy lead into a weighty head. The base of each head had a hole, or eye, into which the wooden haft was tightly wedged.

FEROCIOUS FACTS

● Handles ranged from 12 in (30 cm) to 5 ft (152 cm) long. Longer hafts had shattering force.

● The wooden haft was reinforced with metal or leather to blunt or damage an enemy's sword.

Top Training

Trainees bashed their flails against a small target or moving dummy. Then they practiced against each other using a lightweight wooden version of the weapon.

Super Skills

The end of a knight's flail was either a baton or a spiked ball. The knight swung it constantly with outstretched arms so it did not come back and hit him.

Mighty Materials

Blacksmiths added a steel safety chain to the head of a knight's flail. This kept it from flying off like an uncontrolled missile.

Ferocious Facts

• Two-handed flails were the height of a soldier, up to 6 ft (1.8 m).

• Some flail heads were star-shaped, capable of ripping flesh.

• Peasants used their threshing flails as defensive weapons to protect their fields from crop-raiders and land-grabbers.

FAST, FATAL FLAIL

This vicious, two-handed battering weapon was based on a peasant's powerful threshing tool. Sometimes, peasants fought with it very effectively for their lord or king. The flail's spiked or knobbed baton end was connected by a chain or leather thong to a long haft. This free movement allowed the weapon end to swing with great speed and force. A fighter with fast, accurate aim could kill with a single blow. The baton could hook around weapons, shields, or even knights' bodies and drag them to the ground.

WHERE
Europe

WHEN
1200s to 1500s
—based on earlier
Asian weapons

Baton with metal studs to cause extra damage

Chain attachment

Two-handed haft about 6 ft (1.8 m) long

Beastly Medieval Battleaxe

WHERE
Worldwide

WHEN
800s to 1500s
—based on prehistoric
agricultural tools

These savage axes were sleek and sturdy chopping weapons. Their broad, crescent-shaped blades could slice or sever limbs, halting enemies in their tracks. A single blow could pierce a helmet, plate armor, or shield, or chop off a head. There were single- and double-handed battleaxes, with short, long, and even longer pole hafts. Some had a blade on one side and a curved hammer or pick shape on the other. The battleaxe was a common weapon of the foot soldier, but a knight might tuck a small one in his belt.

- Iron axe head with decorative patterning

- Long haft, inserted into a socket in the butt end of the axe head

TOP TRAINING

Most foot soldiers used an axe from an early age, for chopping wood. Later, they practiced accurate, swift slicing and throwing, probably at tree trunks or wood blocks.

SUPER SKILLS

Skilled soldiers could hook their battleaxes around swords, shields, plate armor, and horses' reins—and around their opponents' legs and ankles to pull them off balance.

MIGHTY MATERIALS

Blacksmiths cast iron battleaxe heads in molds. They then tempered, or softened, the edges with further heating. This made the blades less brittle. Most hafts were wooden, though some were iron.

FEROCIOUS FACTS

- A short haft of 12 in (30 cm) was perfect for close-combat chopping.

- The halberd was a doubly fierce combination of pike and battleaxe.

- Many battleaxes could be thrown at once, to distances of up to 40 ft (12 m), in a rain of blades.

WARS AND WARRIORS

Victory in battle and even in war has often been due to the strength of metal weapons and and devastating use of clever tactics.

PERFECT PIKE FORMATION

One of the most effective tacticians to use the phalanx formation was Epaminondas (about 410–362 BCE). This great general and ruler from the central Greek city of Thebes used it to shatter Sparta's hold over the Greek city-states. His breakthrough came at the Battle of Leuctra in 371 BCE. He adopted the new, deep phalanx formation that used a massive 50 rows of hoplites. His greatest innovation, though, was to place these elite troops on the left flank, traditionally the weaker side. The Spartans came at them from their own stronger, right flank. They were impaled by the phalanx of pikes, and Epaminondas's center units and right flanks cleaned up the rest.

SAVED BY THE WAR FAN

The gunsen and gunbai war fans were weapons of defense as much as attack. They often saved the life of a cornered samurai. This is what happened during the Fourth Battle of Kawanakajima in central Japan, in 1561. It took place between two rival military leaders, Takeda Shingen and Uesugi Kenshin. Thundering ahead on his horse, Kenshin had ridden right through the enemy cavalry. He headed straight for Shingen and thrust his sword at him with great force. But Shingen quickly raised his war fan and deflected the strike. For his great fighting skills, Shingen was known as the Tiger of Kai.

LEARNING LONGBOW TACTICS

England's 9th Earl of Warwick, William de Beauchamp (1237–1298), was a skillful military leader who appreciated the strengths of the longbow. Others did not. They preferred the crossbow, which shot lethal bolts straight and at lightning speed. But the earl showed the longbow's worth during one of England's many attempts to crush their neighbors, the Welsh. At the nighttime Battle of Maes Moydog in 1295, the earl drove his cavalry hard at the Welsh, forcing them into small defensive units. Then he unleashed a heavy shower of longbow arrows, killing many and dispersing the rest. This was one of the early battles that used the longbow to its best advantage.

SUCCESS WITH THE SZABLA

The razor-sharp szabla finished off the Polish hussars' many enemies. This highly trained cavalry carried various weapons. They would charge hard at their enemy, screaming and with their armor flashing, and then strike with their 19-ft (5.8-m) lightweight lances. The hussars followed this by shooting their opponents with pistols or stabbing them with daggers. They delivered single, fatal strikes with the szabla. This strategy led to many successes for the Polish hussars. In 1581, at the Battle of Kircholm, 1,000 hussars charged into 4,000 Swedish infantry, and even cannon! The powerful Swedish army was defeated and cut to bits.

MASTER SWORDFIGHTER

Miyamoto Musashi (1584–1645) was a famous samurai warrior known also as a *kensai*, or "sword saint." He aimed to perfect the art and technique of the killer katana. Musashi fought and won at least 60 fights, slicing to death most of his opponents. This master swordfighter was not content with using just one sword to slash at his enemy. He developed the terrifying technique of *nito ichi-ryu*, wielding a katana in one hand and a short sword in the other. Sometimes Musashi threw the short sword at his opponent, then attacked with the killer katana.

More Ferocious Facts

- Hoplites' spearheads became much heavier in the 4th century. A metal butt at the other end of the haft was needed to balance the spearhead. The butt could also be used as a weapon.

- Horses were often severely wounded or even killed by spears. So, in the 4th century, the Byzantine army protected them with plate armor, just like their cavalrymen.

- At the Battle of Leuctra in 371 BCE, 1,000 mighty Spartans were piked to death by 6,000 Theban hoplites. This marked the beginning of the downfall of Sparta.

- The longbow fired some lethal arrowheads. The most damaging was the hardened steel broadhead arrow. It could be cast with two to four blade edges that ripped into the foe's flesh, causing massive bleeding.

- The mace was used by priests! They were allowed to hit armored knights, so long as no bleeding occurred. An image of the Bishop of Bayeux clutching a mace appears on the Bayeux Tapestry in France. The artwork depicts England's defeat by the French in the Battle of Hastings in 1066.

- Knights did not care about their enemies' horses and pounded their legs with war hammers to make them fall.

- A heavy war hammer from the Middle East called the horseman's pick was designed not to hurt horses. Its long spike end was rammed into enemy armor or thrown.

- At the Battle of Crécy in 1346, English longbowmen faced French crossbow bolts and charging cavalry. But they held their ground, piercing and killing about 12,000 Frenchmen and their allies.

- In 1879, Zulu warriors in South Africa defeated British soldiers at the Battle of Isandhlwana. The British soldiers were heavily outnumbered, but they had rifles, rockets, and mountain guns. The Zulus used spears and a few old muskets. In skilled hands, ancient metal weapons can be very successful, even in recent times.

GLOSSARY

BARBED
Having sharp, hooked tips

CAVALRY
Soldiers on horseback

CROSSBOW
Horizontal bow that shoots bolts straight at an enemy

HILT
Sword handle and pommel

HOPLITE
Ancient Greek pikeman

INFANTRY
Foot soldiers

MOUNTAIN GUN
A gun that can be dismantled and transported uphill

PHALANX
Rows of soldiers holding pikes in close formation

PLATE ARMOR
Body armor made from smooth plates of steel

PRESSURE POINT
A point on the body that feels pain or numbness when pressed hard

SAMURAI
Japanese warrior

SCABBARD
A sheath for holding a sword

SHAFT
The arm of an arrow or spear

WINGED HUSSARS
Heavily armed Polish cavalry who wore wings to look more fearsome

INDEX

THE AUTHOR

Catherine Chambers was born in Adelaide, South Australia, grew up in the UK, and studied African history and Swahili at the School of Oriental and African Studies in London. She has written about 130 books for children and young adults and enjoys seeking out intriguing facts for her nonfiction titles, which cover history, cultures, faiths, biography, geography, and the environment.

THE ILLUSTRATOR

Martín Bustamante is an illustrator and painter from Argentina. As a teenager, he found new and fascinating worlds full of color, shape, and atmosphere in movies such as Star Wars and the comic strip Prince Valiant, and these became his inspiration for drawing. Martin became a professional illustrator and has worked on books and magazines in Argentina, the USA, and Europe.

Picture Credits (abbreviations: t = top; b = bottom; c = center; l = left; r = right)

© www.shutterstock.com: 6 tl, 6 tr, 6 bl, 6 br, 7tc, 7br